THE
ANGEL®
CARDS
BOOK

Inspirational Messages
and Meditations

D1510078

by
Kathy Tyler and Joy Drake

Library of Congress Catalog Card Number: 99-62549
Authors: Tyler, Kathy and Drake, Joy
Title: The ANGEL® Cards Book, Inspirational Messages and Meditations

Editors: Carolyn Kott Washburne, Anne Aufderheide

ISBN: 0-934245-41-X
10 9 8 7 6 5 4 3 2
Published by Narada Productions, Inc.

To the Angels within all of us.

Table of Contents

1

Introduction

We wrote this book in response to the number of requests we have received from people interested in knowing more about the ANGEL® Cards: where they come from, how to use them, and what they might mean.

We have worked extensively with the qualities in the ANGEL Cards deck. We feel that the concept of qualities represents a wide variety of characteristics, attributes, and experiences. We find the ANGEL Cards' qualities can empower us to make changes and support both our inner dialog and our interactions with others to bring about a more conscious response to life. The cards are simple, yet they can hold profound realizations of the spiritual truths that apply to everyday life.

The focus of the ANGEL Cards is to encourage the deepening of our awareness and ability to let our spirits live fully in a materialistic world. Because our inner selves are often less tangible than the events that surround us, it is easy to abandon our intuitive impulses. Yet we have the choice of how, when, and why to interact with a particular situation. Most importantly, we have the choice of how that situation affects us. When we realize this, we can then be effective rather than affected by circumstances. This gives us the opportunity to experience the power of creation as opposed to the disempowerment of random reactions.

One thing we have learned over the years, as our relationship to the Angels has grown, is that if there is no awareness of the possibility of their help, then the connection does not occur. Interest in developing contact with the

Angels allows the relationship to happen. You will find that the more you work with the Angels, the more tangible your inner reality can become.

The ANGEL® Cards can offer a portal of imagination to help us think differently about ourselves, or a part of our lives, and to act in new ways. Our self-love can deepen when we learn to acknowledge and work with our present experience, even when it is not one we would wish. This can empower us to make new decisions and take creative actions. As you explore your connection to the Angels, remember what a quality means at one time in relation to the particular intention; drawing the same Angel at a different time for a different purpose may have quite another meaning.

It is our intention through this publication to support you in exploring your inner wisdom rather than to tell you how to proceed. That is up to your unique process of self-discovery. Angels come to share their light and to help us through our growth periods. Free yourself to follow your intuitive promptings and use your imagination to explore.

Let the Angels inspire you to risk a response to life that is new, spontaneous, and fresh. Allow the Angels to guide you to act in congruence with your highest values and integrity. Our deepest wish for you is that you develop the ability to trust your intuition and live your life from the "inside out."

Kathy Tyler and Joy Drake
Asheville, North Carolina
August 1999

ANGEL® Cards

Creation and History of the ANGEL Cards

The ANGEL Cards were originally designed as part of a board game, The Transformation Game®, by Joy Drake and Kathy Tyler while living at the Findhorn Foundation in Scotland. The Transformation Game and the Findhorn Foundation are described in detail in Chapter 10. The Transformation Game is designed to encourage individual creativity and enhance our ability to interact successfully in relationships. In The Transformation Game cards are drawn in response to a particular issue about which the player is seeking insight.

The purpose of the ANGEL Cards in The Transformation Game is to bring spirit into our everyday lives and to help us find ways to stay in touch with our inner selves. They deepen our exploration and understanding of our beliefs and assist us in reviewing automatic behaviors that may be extensions of those beliefs. The ANGEL Cards provide insightful input into our thought patterns and can bring graceful change by providing fresh perspectives.

The ANGEL Cards are much more than just cards. They have an energy unto themselves. They can help us expand our sensitivity to inner resources and uncover a deeper understanding of personal issues. After exploring many different qualities as possible ANGEL Cards, we came to the current 52 after much attunement and monitoring test games for several months.

We decided to produce the ANGEL® Cards in response to a number of requests from our workshop participants and first offered them for sale in 1981. They were initially printed at the Findhorn Press, and we hand cut and collated them. Soon the cards became a sideline cottage industry in addition to our full-time educational work. The ANGEL Cards rapidly became a part of the Findhorn Foundation Community and its programs, complementing the educational process and personal development of the members and many guests.

While we were in the United States offering Transformation Game workshops, we met the folks at Narada Productions, Inc., in Milwaukee, Wisconsin. That was the beginning of a lasting relationship. In 1981, Narada began to produce and distribute the ANGEL Cards. Currently the ANGEL Cards have been translated into Dutch, German, French, and Spanish. Over a million card sets have been sold worldwide.

Essence of the ANGEL Cards

We call them ANGEL Cards because they represent pure essences. Meditating on them brings support to help you overcome obstacles and gain greater understanding of your inner self.

ANGEL Cards offer an opportunity to deepen wisdom, strengthen self-knowledge, and connect with your inner light. Each card illustrates a keynote quality that can evoke your intuitive ability to discern the next step. The Angels are inner companions that support growth and bring understanding and direction. They are qualities of aliveness that can assist and encourage an experience of life at a deeper level.

It is important to realize that the ANGEL Cards' qualities are not polarities. Each individual card includes a spectrum of experience. The words may appear to be in the positive form. However, once you begin to work deeply with a quality, you may soon experience its opposite expression. You may realize that to experience and share the positive expression, you need to become aware of the negative or opposite expression. To understand our experiences, we need to become aware of our many-layered selves. For example, if you select the Angel of Play, rather than pleasurable involvement in your daily activities, you may realize you are stressed with the effort of completing tasks. In this way, the ANGEL Cards can be used to reflect on your values and choices, training your mind to touch the source of creation.

When selecting qualities for the week ahead, the entire month, or a particular meeting, we discover that Angels can give us the opportunity to reevaluate our behaviors and make new choices. They can inspire us to find new ways of being and acting that enhance our life force rather than diminish it. The Angels can help us discover supportive, encouraging, and life-giving circumstances, as well as deepen our self-acceptance and our ability to respect ourselves and become congruent with what we believe and how we act.

Through the support and assistance of the Angels, we have the opportunity to explore and experience becoming an integrated whole being. And in doing so, areas in need of healing are often revealed. A useful technique is to act "as if" you are already that which you desire to be. For example, if you select the Angel of Responsibility, you begin to act as though you are a responsible person and also treat those around you as responsible individuals. When you act "as if," you find new ways to emulate your understanding of that particular way of being. In so doing, you learn new ways to behave, and you move beyond the responses and choices you have made in the past. Each moment becomes a creative moment, a moment of choice rather than a moment to repeat past reactions to handle current tensions or challenges. With the assistance of the Angels we can learn to develop wisdom from the past, not repeat it. This, of course, requires diligence, a willingness to be vulnerable, and the ability to stay open to the moment. It requires us to be engaged and live life from the "inside out," in other words, to be fully present to ourselves, our experience, and our environment.

Choosing an ANGEL® Card

ANGEL Cards are simple to work with, and there are an infinite number of ways to use them. Each of the 52 cards has a playfully illustrated keyword to help you focus on a particular aspect of your inner life. The more you think about the quality reflected by the word and picture on the card, the more you will find this quality echoing in your life.

You can pick a card at the beginning of a new cycle or venture; you can choose one with a particular task in mind, an obstacle to overcome, or simply to give you a direction to focus on for a certain period of time. The clearer your intention and the more serious your approach, the more powerful your choice of cards will be. Part of your being knows what you need and will reach for it. This is why it is important to accept and work with whatever quality comes to you, even if you do not immediately understand it.

Angels come to share their light and to help us with our growth periods. You can request the assistance of the Angels in a variety of situations. For example you can:

- Choose an Angel on your birthday as a keynote for your new year, or on other special occasions.
- Select a daily or weekly Angel to bring inspiration to work, school, family, or relationships.
- Pick an Angel with a friend or relative with whom you would like deeper communication.
- Choose an Angel for a person who is at a distance and in need of healing. Just think of that person and select an Angel for him or her. Then picture that person supported by, and radiant with, the Angel you selected.

In most situations absorbing and working with one Angel quality effectively provides the support and guidance you need. However, when it feels appropriate to draw a second or third ANGEL® Card, feel free to follow your intuitive promptings and use your imagination to explore the cards.

Guidelines for Use

Find a quiet place where you will not be disturbed. Light a candle or dim the lights to give a soft feeling to the room. Shuffle the ANGEL Cards and arrange them face down on a tray or table in a pleasing pattern in front of you.

Use one of the meditations in this book to connect with and welcome an Angel. You may also use the following suggested creative visualization, or another meditation that you prefer. You may want to make an audio recording of the meditations so that you can listen to them as you choose Angels.

Read through the visualization once or twice, noting the main points. Then give the process a try.

Visualization

Preparation

Sit down comfortably. Close your eyes. Breathe slowly and deeply. Relax. Take time to allow your emotions to become calm, and let your mind be open and receptive. In this quiet, relaxed state reflect on your present life situation. Direct your attention to a particular period of time or issue of concern with which you would like assistance and insight. Focus on one specific situation or goal that is important to you at this time. As you concentrate steadily on this issue, affirm your willingness to accept support and make changes in your life.

Decide if you will be selecting one Angel or using a spread of Angels. Decide on the time frame, a day, a week, or a month, that you will work with the Angel. Take a few moments to write down your intention for choosing a card. What is it you hope to clarify, heal, or release? Be as specific as you can. The more specific you are in your intention for requesting the Angel, the clearer the response and participation of the Angel.

Connection

Inwardly invite an Angel to join you. Imagine a contact being made and a pure stream of light from above illuminating your present situation. Allow the comfort of this presence to embrace and surround you, lifting and expanding your awareness. Open to it fully. Take time to let this connection strengthen and deepen. When you feel ready, simply open your eyes and select a card.

Communication

Take time to look at the Angel selected, reflecting on the keyword. Open this book to the inspirational message for the Angel you have chosen. This can be used as a starting point to begin to connect with your Angel. Then close your eyes once again and move back into the silence and welcome your Angel by name. Invite its purity and radiance to infuse your situation. Open your heart and mind to communication with your Angel, and allow the significance of the quality to become conscious.

Ask your Angel to suggest practical ways you can express this quality in your current situation. Let your Angel speak to you through images, feelings, or words. Listen carefully. Begin to apply your insight by deciding where and how you can bring this quality into your present situation. Choose one action you will take to achieve this.

If you decided to select multiple cards, repeat the connection and communication process for each one.

Affirmation

Affirm your ability to be a clear, open expression for each quality. Visualize each Angel flowing into your life in creative and harmonious ways. Picture yourself giving and receiving each quality with radiant results, including the situation about which you are inquiring.

Gifts and Thanksgiving

Finally, ask for a gift from your Angel and take whatever reveals itself - picture, feeling, or phrase. Recalling this gift will summon your Angel and reconnect you with its presence.

Close the visualization by giving thanks, in your own way, for the insight and inspiration from your Angel.

Completion

When you feel ready, open your eyes. Make a note of each Angel you have chosen and write down ways your Angel can assist you in improving your situation. Record your impressions and ideas before moving on. Note the action you have chosen to take.

You may wish to return to a reflective, quiet space and dialogue with the Angel in subsequent days, becoming aware of how your goals are being fulfilled. It is helpful to keep a daily record in your journal, noting to what extent you have consciously expressed the healing power of the quality to yourself, to others and to your environment.

When you intuitively feel that it is time to choose a new Angel, begin by acknowledging the contribution each current Angel has made to your life. Then release it with your appreciation, allowing the Angel to move on before you begin the selection of a new one.

Use the ANGEL® Cards Journal on page 56 to keep track of your experiences.

3

Choosing More Than One ANGEL® Card

Choosing two ANGEL Cards can have a synergistic effect. The following suggestions are just a few of the many ideas for card spreads.

Two-Card Spread

A two-card spread can provide insight and perspective that may not be revealed without both Angels as reminders.

For example, if you pick the Angels of Delight and Patience, a new feeling emerges. When you experience Delight and Patience together (being patient with a sense of delight toward what is going on in your life), your experience is different than if you choose the Angels of Delight and Purification. Choosing these two qualities together may assist you in clearing clutter with pleasure.

The procedure for choosing two Angels is similar to selecting a single ANGEL Card. The essential first step, as with all the ANGEL Card processes, is formulating a clear intention. Through the support of two Angels, what is it you hope to clarify, heal, or release? Clarify your intention and write it down before proceeding.

Follow the basic visualization outline on page 13 and invite two Angels to assist you. Select two ANGEL Cards and take time to reflect on both qualities in unison.

Sometimes it is helpful to use two Angels sequentially. Choose the first Angel for a quality you can bring into your present situation. For example, if you chose the Angel of Harmony for your present situation, it might suggest that you reflect on where Harmony is now, or maybe what part of yourself can respond harmoniously to what is going on now. You would then act from that part of yourself.

Next, choose a second Angel for a direction you might bring to the same situation. For example, if the second Angel you select is Compassion, this might indicate a need to move toward a state of compassion, with the Angel of Harmony as your usher. In other words, by experiencing a state of harmony within yourself and bringing it to your current situation, the circumstances would then allow compassion to be felt or shared. The feeling of compassion would be an indication that you were acting with your intention in mind. If you did not experience compassion, either in yourself or the situation, this might indicate that you were not achieving your intention. You could then reevaluate your actions to determine if there is any place where harmony would be helpful. Then decide how you could bring more harmony into your circumstance until you begin to feel compassion.

Use the ANGEL® Cards Journal on page 56 to keep track of your experiences.

Three-Card Spread

A three-card spread allows you to work with a timeline to gain perspective and insight into your situation or concern.

Begin by formulating a clear, specific intention. What is it you hope to clarify, heal, or release through the support of three Angels? Clarify your intention and write it down before proceeding further.

- The first Angel addresses the past. Take time to explore the past interactions and events related to your intention.

    How was this Angel quality a part of these events?
    Where could the Angel have been more active, and what happened to block this quality?
    What lesson does the past hold from which you can gain wisdom?

- The second Angel addresses the present, reflecting the quality that can be most helpful in experiencing the truth of what is happening now. You may need to reevaluate your assumptions, judgments, or predetermined decisions that have limited you in some way.

    Where is this quality expressed in the here and now?
    Where is this quality blocked from expression now?
    How can you bring this quality into your intention now?
    Is there any change of behavior or action you need to take to be more congruent with your values?

- The third Angel addresses the future, inviting the quality that you ideally intend to manifest.

    What is the underlying essence of the outcome you wish for?
    How can you apply your wisdom to future interactions?
    What action will bring this quality into your life more directly?

Use the ANGEL® Cards Journal on page 56 to keep track of your experiences.

Multiple-Card Spread

You can draw an ANGEL Card for every person involved in your concern. You would then relate to each person specifically though the characteristics of each Angel. This can help to bridge differences and allow you to move toward resolution.

Keep it simple by picking cards only for the "main players" in your situation. If you do this particular exercise, remember the Angel that has come for each relationship and consciously bring that quality into your interaction with the person. Also, look for the Angel to express through the person, that is, for the person to manifest the quality of the Angel, even if only in a subtle way. When this happens, follow the flow of the energy. You might find this challenging if you are not open to changing your perception of the person or situation and your part in creating it.

The Angels can support and assist you in shifting your attitude and experiencing your life differently. This requires your participation and willingness to be aware of this inner support. It also requires your willingness to let go of your predetermined decisions about how you expect yourself or another person to act. It is in the moment that new inspiration comes; trusting your intuition takes practice. Giving yourself permission to experiment and learn can be a very rewarding experience.

Use the ANGEL® Cards Journal on page 56 to keep track of your experiences.

Combination Blessing, Angel, and Insight Spread

Throughout the course of our work with the ANGEL Cards, we developed tools that have a synergistic effect when used together. Please refer to the Products in Chapter 10 for further information.

Overview

In this section we use a combination of card decks in a creative process designed to deepen our understanding of the interconnectedness of daily events. Adding Blessing Cards™ and Insight Cards to your ANGEL Cards can clarify and expand your realizations. This exercise is used to enhance and deepen your relationships. The process is a way to share your energy with people and situations that concern you. It can help you focus on healing thoughts and assist you to open up to the highest outcomes. You may want to include this process as part of your morning meditation. You may also place focus cards on your altar, or wherever you have created a special area for spiritual attunement, as a reminder of your higher intentions.

Preparation

For the combination spread outlined below you will need:
- A deck of ANGEL Cards
- A bowl of Blessing Cards™ (see page 76)
- A deck of Insight Cards from an Intuitive Solutions® set (see page 76)
- About 2 dozen 3″-x-5″ index cards.

Begin by identifying the areas of your life to which you would like to direct your energy, insight, and blessing. "Focus cards" allow you to concentrate on a person, situation, or goal that is important to you. Take several 3″-x-5″ cards and on each card write the name of that person, situation, or goal. You may want to include family members, friends, colleagues, or pets. You might like to focus on your health; the emotional, mental, intuitive, and spiritual aspects of yourself; your work or hobbies; or an upcoming meeting or vacation. There may also be local issues or community, national, or global situations that are in your heart at this time.

It is also helpful to label at least three cards as "Special." This allows you the freedom to choose, in the moment, a new focus area that is not already on one of your cards. Shuffle the 3"-x-5" focus cards and place them face down in front of you. Sit quietly for a few moments. Consolidate your energy. Let go of future and past thinking and become fully present. Take a moment to appreciate the opportunity you have to make a difference. Open your heart to the life you are creating and to those who are part of it. Let your gratitude flow out and acknowledge all of those people and places that are part of your life.

Step 1: Focusing

From an empty, receptive space hold the intention that you will select for those people, places, or situations that can benefit most from your attention and blessing at this time. Then choose three focus cards and place them, face up, in a row in front of you.

Step 2: Blessing

Place the Blessing Cards in a bowl.

- Take a few moments and think about the first focus area. Ask yourself, What blessing can I bring to this person, situation, or process now? Next, choose a Blessing card. Place the Blessing you choose on the first focus card. See that aspect of your life, person, or situation enriched by this particular Blessing. Move on to your second focus area and repeat the procedure. Finally, choose a Blessing for your third focus area.

- Now return to the first focus card and choose a second Blessing for that focus area. Ask yourself, What blessing will enhance my relationship with this person, situation, or process now? Place the second Blessing you select next to the first Blessing on the 3"-x-5" card. Move on to your second focus area and repeat the procedure. Finally, choose a Blessing for your third focus area.

- Sit quietly and close your eyes. Let the energy of your selected Blessings stream in turn to each focus area, blessing each person/situation/aspiration as well as your relationship to each of them. Visualize this blessing happening in wonderful and life-affirming ways. Stay open to insights that may spontaneously arise.

Step 3: Angels

Shuffle the ANGEL® Cards deck.

Think about your first focus area. Invite and select an ANGEL Card to carry your blessings to this first destination and to enhance your relationship to it. Place the ANGEL Card you select above the first focus card. Then move on to your second focus area. Select an Angel to infuse this area and place the ANGEL Card you select above the second focus card. Finally, choose an Angel for the third focus area and place the ANGEL Card you select above the third focus card.

Take a few moments to imagine each focus area being blessed with the pure quality of the Angel you selected. Stay open to insights that may spontaneously arise.

Step 4: Insights

Shuffle the Insight deck from the Intuitive Solutions® set.

Concentrate on your first focus area. Move into a space where you are one with the Angel you selected for it. As the Angel of _____ (the card you selected), look at the person, situation, or process in your focus and, from that place select an Insight Card that offers the maximum clarity, benefit, or direction at this time.

Take a few moments to absorb the message of the Insight you have drawn, then move on to your second focus area and repeat the Insight procedure. Finally, choose an Insight Card to anchor the energy for your third focus area.

Step 5: Commitment

Sit quietly and inwardly affirm your willingness to stay open to input from these three Angels for the next 24 hours, and to recognize opportunities to give and receive blessings. Invite inspiration during this time and offer your prayers for the well being of everyone involved, and for the Earth.

Step 6: Closure

Make a note of the Blessings, Angels, and Insight Cards you drew for each focus area, and any thoughts, feelings, or messages that the text prompts. The cards that you draw may touch you very powerfully or poignantly. Follow your feelings to derive the maximum benefit from them. Alternately, if you are puzzled by any of the cards you have drawn, be patient. A clear message may be apparent immediately — but if not, do not over analyze. Instead, let the text of the cards move more deeply within you over the next 24 hours. Ask for interactions, life situations, and your dreams to bring you understanding of the cards without effort or strain. Continue to imagine the focus area to be blessed each time you think of it over the next 24 hours.

Use the Combination Blessing, Angel, and Insight Journal on page 64 to keep track of your experiences.

4

Choosing Angels In
Group Settings

This process is written with group facilitators in mind. This section includes guidelines for the facilitator as well as suggestions for "scripts" to be read aloud to the group.

Choose ANGEL® Cards, for example, at the beginning of a workshop, class, retreat, or conference and use them for the duration of the program. You can also choose Angels at the end of the group time to assist in integrating the experience into each individual's daily life.

Preparation

Facilitator: Set out the ANGEL Cards face down on a table or a tray. Let the arrangement be clean, orderly, and beautiful. Take whatever time you need before the group begins to focus on the purpose for the meeting. Connect with your current Angel or remember an inspirational highlight you had with an Angel that was uplifting and insightful. Be open to a creative, intuitive experience that can focus the meeting. Allow yourself to be mindful and willing to be of the highest service to the group.

Introduction

Facilitator: Give some background about The Transformation Game® from which the ANGEL Cards come. The following script may be useful.

Script Suggestion
  The Transformation Game is a powerful, dynamic transformational tool. The experience of playing the game helps us to see ourselves more

clearly through its objective lens. We can move through the doorway the game provides to an expanded inner life and from that point to creating a more satisfying and peaceful outer life. As well as bringing greater self-understanding, the game also enables groups to work with higher consciousness and in harmony with one another.

In the game the ANGEL® Cards act as triggers to catalyze an inner experience. They expand our sensitivity, drawing our attention to an aspect within that we may not have been aware of before, or to one that is very familiar to us — whatever is most needed for our spiritual development at the time. Part of our being knows what we need and will reach for it. The next step is to integrate that quality into our daily lives in ways that help us to achieve our intentions in alignment with the highest good for all.

Set Up the Process

Facilitator: Ask members of the group to release their expectations and relax into the flow of the guided meditation. Invite them to simply be receptive to their inner impressions, images, and feelings as they appear. Reassure them that there is no wrong or right experience.

The process occurs basically in two steps. The first is a guided meditation to clarify our intentions and allow the Angels to enter the group. The second step allows each person to deepen his or her individual connection to the Angels in unique and creative ways.

Script Suggestion

First, we will move into the silence and get in touch with our intentions for choosing an Angel. Next, there will be a guided meditation in which we will invite the Angels to be with us. As each person feels ready, we will each choose an ANGEL Card we feel drawn to. If someone else chooses the card you were drawn to, simply recenter yourself and choose again. Once everyone has chosen a card, we will go around the group and everyone will share the name of the quality that is on his or her card. Then, we will return to the silence and consciously deepen our connection with the Angel we have chosen. Finally, we will find a partner and share our insights and experience with that person before returning to the larger group.

Facilitator: When everyone has understood the basic format, explain that you will be choosing an Angel to overlight the whole group and to act as a point of unification and inspiration throughout our time together.

Part 1: The Guided Meditation

Facilitator instructions are highlighted in *italics* throughout this guided meditation.

Script Suggestion

Close your eyes. Get comfortable. Breathe slowly and deeply and relax. Let your emotions settle and your mind become still and open. Now get in touch with your current life situation and begin to focus on those aspects of yourself or your environment that you would like to change or improve. *Pause.* What do you intend to create and contribute to this group? Clarify your personal goals for our time together. Affirm your willingness for your intention to be fulfilled and realize the changes it may involve for you.

Pause for a moment and allow time for participants to reflect.

Experience this clear intention filling your awareness slowly and gradually until you are holding your attention fully and steadily on this intention. *Pause.* We ask that our intentions be aligned with the highest good for all, and we now open ourselves to the presence of the Angels. We invite an Angel to join each one here as a companion on his or her chosen path for this time together.

Feel or imagine a pure stream of energy entering your being. Feel it surrounding you and breathe it in. Let it fill you, lifting and expanding your awareness. *Pause.* When you feel that the contact has been made, take time to let it strengthen. Then, in your own time, let it guide you to the card that will reveal the name of the quality you have chosen. When you are ready, simply open your eyes and quietly select an ANGEL® Card.

Once everyone has chosen a card, go around the group and share the names of the Angels. Then move back into the silence.

Welcome your Angel. Feel its purity and radiance filling you. Open up the lines of communication and let your Angel speak to you in words, images, or feelings. Listen deeply and follow the first impressions that come. *Pause*. Now be open to receiving a gift from your Angel. Take whatever presents itself, a message, picture, symbol, or feeling to strengthen your connection to this quality. *Pause*. Finally, visualize yourself as a clear, open expression for this quality into this group. Imagine your Angel's essence flowing gracefully through you in new, creative, and harmonious ways. *Pause*. Let us give thanks for the many blessings of spirit and hold this special energy in our hearts as we return our awareness to the room to share with one another.

Part 2: Sharing in Partners

Script Suggestion

Choose a partner. Find a place in the room where you can talk quietly together.

Wait until everyone has found a partner before continuing with the instructions. If there is an odd number, either join in yourself or take time to make a threesome.

Each person will take three minutes *(or whatever time you decide to allow)*. Decide who will go first. The first partner will begin with sharing insights, understanding, and messages from his or her Angel while the other partner listens without interrupting, giving full attention. Then, if there is time after the sharing partner is finished, the listening partner can offer any insights that might have occurred.

Call "time" when the partners should change over. When both partners have shared, ask all group members to finish up and, remaining where they are sitting, move into the silence once again.

Visualize your partner sitting in front of you. Imagine your partner accepting and expressing his or her Angel easily, clearly, and fully. See your partner's inner beauty flowing out, into his or her life, uplifting everyone. Now allow your attention to expand and include the entire group in your awareness. Let us open to and welcome the presence of an Angel to be with our group for the time we are together. *Pause while you move quietly to the tray and choose the group Angel.*

Let us welcome the Angel of _____ into our group and open ourselves to a personal connection with this Angel. We invite this quality to fill our hearts and minds, linking us and lifting us up. Be open to the group Angel now and let it speak to you. Take a moment to reflect on your connection with the group Angel and your personal Angel. How do they blend together for you? *Pause*. Now silently affirm your willingness to contribute your part in the group during our time together, allowing this quality to express itself fully.

Gently open your eyes and return your awareness to the room. Move back to the large group, and we will take some time to share together.

Group Sharing

Facilitator: Ask the group members to share, depending on the time you have allowed. Encourage everyone to share as they are inspired, either about the group Angel or his or her personal Angel in relation to their intention.

If someone asks you what his or her Angel means, let that person know that no one else can interpret the card. However, you can assist by reading the inspirational message for its quality from Chapter 5 of this book. If someone does not understand the significance of an Angel, suggest that he or she ask to be shown, over the next couple of days, what the quality means by listening, staying alert, and being patient.

Next Steps and Follow-Up

Script Suggestion

Follow-up is very important. Choosing an ANGEL® Card does not guarantee instant transformation! You will need to keep in touch with your Angel throughout the time you wish to work with the quality. Dialogue with your Angel in meditation. Build a relationship. Share your challenges, insights, and gratitude. Use your Angel as an inner friend and valuable resource. Take time to review what part this quality has played in your interactions, noticing areas of improvement.

When you are finished working with this quality, release your Angel with gratitude. Before choosing a new ANGEL Card, always take time to clarify your intention for working with an Angel. Also, always accept and work with whatever quality comes, finding its gift. If you do not, the power leaves the process, the Angels become less impactful, and the insights are not as deep.

With regular use of the ANGEL® Cards you can draw angelic energy into your life and apply their inspiration to challenges and changes along your path.

Final Blessing

Facilitator: Close the process with this final blessing.

Script Suggestion

Feel the presence of your Angel and the group's Angel. Let these qualities fill you until you are full of their light and blessing. Then breathe them out into the group, community, and planet. Continue to fill and breathe out. *Pause.* We hold the Earth in light and love and blessing. Thank you.

5

Inspirational Messages
Of The ANGEL® Cards

Your life experience and knowledge are unique. Using ANGEL Cards can reinforce the wisdom you have gained and encourage continuous growth. Let the Angels support your ability to learn and release outdated decisions and behaviors that may no longer apply.

Use the inspirational messages as a way to become open to the Angel that you choose. Remember, it is not the entire message your Angel will bring you. Each time you select an Angel, approach the process with a beginner's mind, as if each time is the first. Become receptive to new possibilities, willing to suspend your previous notions and allow what is now meaningful to emerge.

The following messages are offered to assist you in accessing your inner wisdom. They are not intended to define in detail or thoroughly explain the Angels. Instead, as a source of inspiration and creativity, each message can be used as a starting point or seed thought to connect with the Angels. There are infinite possibilities of the Angels' messages to you. Be open to the limitless potential.

The qualities are not static; they are multidimensional and multilayered. Each Angel quality is a hologram of the spectrum of energy it represents. There is not a beginning or an end to their meanings, or a right way to express them. The Angels carry with them a depth of wisdom that can move you beyond limited thinking if you open up to the possibility that all you know is not all there is to know.

Cultivate an attitude of generosity and act as though there is plenty for you and for everyone, everywhere. Give freely and generously.

Your life is a grand adventure. Take risks. Explore the unknown. Journey forth into the great, wide open without preplanned outcomes.

Hold a point of steadiness and moderation. Find a point of equilibrium and peaceful coexistence in the midst of change.

The beauty of nature can only be perceived with a serene mind and harmless heart. So, too, is it with the beauty of people.

Birth marks the shift from one dimension to another. New life, new ideas, new forms come into being.

Clear your perceptions free of confusion. Focus on intent and straightforward expression. See the world as it is without your projections, judgments, and assumptions.

A vital link between your interior experience and outward expression. Willingness to share your feelings and thoughts can engage you in more meaningful relationships to yourself, others, and your environment.

Heartfelt understanding of the human condition that encompasses the pain in oneself and others, dissolves judgment, and opens the way for acceptance. Sincere desire to alleviate suffering.

Face what it is in front of you squarely and fearlessly. Discover the truth held in your heart and act on it.

Life is a creative process with many possibilities. Move beyond any preconceived thoughts, feelings, and beliefs, and engage with your unique expression now.

An approach of childlike innocence and freshness. Bring pleasure and enchantment to each relationship, event, and task of everyday life.

Cultivate your ability to learn from life's rich patterns. You may not be able to establish the curriculum, but you can elect what courses to take at any given time and how to apply your knowledge.

Wise use of energy, resources, and time. It may not be the shortest route from point to point, but the most inclusive and effective.

Be present with zestful alertness! Loosen your constraints and let your passion for life uplift others and generate new opportunities.

Your attitude toward the present builds your experience of the future. Hold a positive outlook. Stay miracle-minded and open to surprises.

The unshakable knowing of the heart when nothing makes sense to the mind. Optimism is an expression of faith in action.

Ability to course correct without losing sight of the goal. Let go of narrow-mindedness, stay open to the flow, and keep current with new information.

Let go of resentments, judgments, and fears, and reduce your investment in staying hurt or angry. To forgive is to live in a world that is at peace with human nature.

You are free to change your experience by changing the criteria upon which you base your decisions. Let go of old trappings and express your uniqueness.

Poise and elegance in form, attitude, and action. Give up struggle and allow the universe to participate in the creation of your life.

To be thankful widens the expression of your heart, and increases your ability to nourish the good in and around you.

Listen to the highest rhythm of all the elements and bring them into concert with your essential nature. Conduct your life accordingly.

Let go of the woundedness that separates you from your wholeness, and restore the balance of your true nature.

Self-reflection is an opportunity to acknowledge and honor your truth. Give voice to your genuineness and share your authenticity with those around you.

Your built-in stress reliever. Sprinkle it liberally to lighten and widen your perspective. Let it move you out of the drama of your life.

Create margins in your life for intuitive promptings. Go beyond the daily noise and connect with the source that nourishes all life.

Stand up for what you believe in. Act in congruence with your values and follow through on your commitments.

Approach life with a buoyant attitude, light heart, and unencumbered mind. Let joy lift your spirit and fill each moment.

Let your spiritual nature illuminate and brighten each day. Pay attention! Brushing over details can create gray and stagnant areas.

The essence of contentment and the foundation of serenity. Love is the activation of your spirit reaching out to make connections. It overcomes grief, harbors no ill will, and heals all separation.

What part of you is in charge? Be mindful of your inner knowing. Follow your deepest impulse with discipline and decisiveness.

Let go of predetermined outcomes and guarded responses. Move with receptivity and readiness to change.

Be fully available to the present and bring all of your attention to what is actually happening now. Relax into the flow of life.

A deep sense of belonging and calm abiding. Cultivate a state of equanimity. Rest in tranquility free from attachment and aversion.

Maximize every moment of aliveness. Experience pleasurable involvement in all your activities and enjoy what you are doing. Have fun!

The capacity to act on your awareness with loving discernment. Utilize your resources to the fullest and create win-win experiences.

Let a shower of light cleanse your thoughts, feelings, and actions. Wash away the drama that covers your essential nature.

Clarify what you want and align your actions with the desired results. Live with vision, intention, and determination.

Let go of all that keeps you in the past or takes you into the future. This may include expectations, inhibitions, control, worry, or an outdated self-image.

The ability to respond to life as a series of personal decisions. Staying accountable for your actions strengthens your freedom to choose and builds self-respect.

Simply be yourself. Look past the fanfare and drama to what is enduring. Take time to clarify what is important to you and let nonessentials fall away.

View humanity as your extended family and reach out with acts of kindness to all you meet.

The ability to act appropriately and without hesitation in an unplanned moment. Follow your intuitive promptings and explore the full spectrum of your creativity.

The ability to take action regardless of the outer pressures. Measure your strength by the degree to which you are willing to remain true to your values and risk the unknown.

The ability to be with what is going on rather than remaining preoccupied with what might, should, or could happen. Let go of the need to manage life and deepen into the peace of acceptance.

Act with a win-win attitude. Use your creativity and sensitivity to blend all the diverse parts into a unified whole.

Take actions that reflect the wisdom of your heart. Give generously and freely, and treat yourself and others with kindness and caring.

Change happens when you take responsibility for your awareness and apply it to your everyday life, small moment by small moment.

Move from a place of knowing within you rather than as a result of adaptation to outer experience. Let go of your assumptions and need to control life's creative process.

Truth is an unfolding process that deepens as your wisdom increases. Live in a way that fosters your enduring and direct encounter with life.

The ability to include a deeper comprehension of life in your interactions rather than simply transferring your knowledge from one experience to another. Act with sincerity and empathy.

Willingness

Approach life with an open mind and a how-can-we-make-it-work attitude. Use your will skillfully to enhance the creative process rather than inhibit it.

6

Meditations With The
ANGEL® Cards

Weekly Meditation

Find a quiet place to sit where you will not be disturbed. Lay out the ANGEL Cards face down in a pleasing pattern so you can see every card. As you do this, begin to think about why you want to choose an Angel at this time.

Take a moment to clarify your intention for the coming week. Look for what is most stimulating or has the most energy for you as you think about it. Form your thoughts into a clear statement and write it down.

Sit comfortably and close your eyes. Take a couple of relaxing breaths. Calm your thoughts and feelings. Bring into your awareness your intention for the coming week. Imagine it being fulfilled in ways you may not plan. Feel what it would be like to have your intention successfully met.

Now invite the presence of an Angel to join you. Allow a contact to be made. Feel or imagine an Angel connecting with you. Open to its presence. Let it fill you and strengthen your intention.

When you are ready, open your eyes and allow yourself to be drawn to an ANGEL Card. Turn it over. Read the inspirational message for this particular Angel in Chapter 5. Then return to the silence with the inspirational message as your seed thought.

Welcome the presence of the Angel that has joined you. Take a moment of quiet and allow this Angel to bring you its message. It may be in words or images. It may be a memory or a new thought. Stay with whatever occurs first. Reflect for a moment and allow any meaning it may hold to become clearer.

Now feel or imagine the presence of your Angel moving into the coming week. Experience the Angel as a companion along your path, assisting and supporting the highest potential to unfold and become your experience. What is the part you need to play for this to happen? Again, follow the first thought, feeling, or image that comes to you. Are you prepared to do your part? Is there a commitment you might make now that would connect you more deeply to your Angel?

During the week remember to connect with your Angel and your intention. Look for its presence throughout the week. Not only will the Angel express itself through your actions, but also through the actions of others. Remember, the more you consciously open to the Angel's presence, the more you will receive it.

Use the ANGEL® Cards Journal on page 56 to keep track of your experiences.

Relationship Meditation

You can use the ANGEL Cards to assist you in relationships. Draw a card to support you and a partner, friend, business associate, family member, or anyone for whom you would like the support of the Angels.

This meditation is for inviting an Angel to help support you in relating to the person in your heart. It is not to be used to influence the other person or in any way bring an Angel into his or her experience. This meditation is for you to find this quality within you, and within the expression between you and the other person.

Take a moment to think about the relationship that you would like to clarify, heal, release, deepen, or move to its next stage. Clarify your intention for choosing an Angel for this relationship. Keep in mind that we do not always know what is for the highest good of others or ourselves. It may take an act of surrender to get in touch with what might be the best and highest outcome in relation to this other person.

Clarify your intention and write it down. Take a moment to welcome the presence of the Angels and visualize this person with you. Imagine how your intention will work out and feel this intention as it moves through you and out into the relationship. As you move into the dynamic of the relationship, let your intention shift and change appropriately. Perhaps it gets clearer and more specific, or maybe it becomes more general and all-encompassing.

Now invite an Angel to come through you into this relationship, asking for the highest support for all involved. Holding your intention, choose an ANGEL® Card.

Take a moment to look at the card and notice your first thoughts. Read the inspirational message for this particular ANGEL Card in Chapter 5. Then close your eyes and welcome your Angel with the inspirational message as your seed thought. Feel the Angel quality coming into this relationship, into your interactions, and into the silence. As you welcome your Angel into your heart, let it show you what its meaning is for you at this time. Take the first thought, feeling, or image that comes. Let yourself explore any memories, associations, and pictures that arise as fully as you can. Now ask the Angel to show you the best next step for you to take regarding this relationship. Ask how to hold yourself inside to achieve your intention and allow the highest to emerge.

Visualize this quality streaming into the relationship and your surroundings, into the space between you and the other individual. Relax and breathe into this space. Over the next few days allow the Angel's presence to unfold into this space.

Gently open your eyes and make any notes you would like. Make a special note of your best next step and the action that you will take. It may involve only you or it may involve the other person, or both of you.

Use the Relationship Angels Journal on page 57 to keep track of your experiences.

New Year or Birthday Meditation

A new year is a commonly shared time to reflect on what the past year has brought and what your hopes and goals are for the coming year. You might think more in terms of your outer life intentions, for example, your work and professional life, or your relationships and family life.

Birthdays are our personal new year and bring a different kind of reflective time with them, more inwardly focused on who we are and how we are living our lives. Birthdays tend to inspire us to think about the deeper meaning of our life and our mortality as human beings.

Take some time to reflect on the past year and what you would like to bring into the coming year. Be aware of what has been working for you, as well as what you would like to change. Make some notes to remind you of your thoughts.

Now clarify what you would like to achieve during the coming year. Write down three intentions, using the journal pages in Chapter 7. We suggest you begin your statement with the words "I intend to." Be as specific as you can with each of your intentions. Beginning with "I intend to" gives a clear direction for your will to act in congruence with your spirit.

Using a meditative process, you will be choosing three ANGEL® Cards as keynote qualities for your specific intentions for the year ahead. Hold your first intention in your mind and heart as you invite an Angel to join you in achieving the highest good held within this intention. Then, as you feel inspired, choose an ANGEL Card. Take a moment to read the inspirational message for the Angel from Chapter 5, then look inside yourself as you recall your intention and let your intuition open to this quality. Follow your first impression; reflect on its meaning. Remember, you will be working with this intention and this Angel for a year, and the meaning will develop and mature over time. Write down your initial insights on your journal page.

Proceed to your next intention and repeat the process. We have suggested that you have three intentions for the coming year. More than this may disperse your energy and dilute outcomes. However, if you feel it appropriate to have more or less, adjust the process to fit your need.

This process requires your participation. We suggest you take time once a week or once a month to review your intentions and connect with each Angel. As the year goes on, your intention may evolve; aspects that you were unaware were part of your intention may become clearer. Continue to work with your Angel and allow yourself to follow the inspiration you receive. It can be very helpful to share your intentions with supportive friends and to keep a journal of your experience. Over time your inspirations become your wisdom.

Use the New Year Angels Journal on page 58 and Birthday Angels Journal on page 60 to keep track of your experiences.

Nature Walk Meditation

Life is not made up of separate events but of flows and cycles. You can use the Nature Walk Meditation when you feel out of sync with life around you. The Angels can support you in getting in touch with the rhythm of nature and the natural unfoldment of a greater plan or a bigger picture.

Begin by reflecting on a feeling of separateness that occurred as a result of an experience you had. Perhaps you were disempowered in some way, or you did not understand what part you played in creating a feeling of separation. Where is your energy stuck? Where do your thoughts keep returning? Formulate a question and phrase it in such a way that an answer can bring movement to the situation. For example, what attitude or perception do I need to shift to restore a feeling of harmony?

Once you have written your question down, spread your ANGEL® Cards out into a pattern in front of you. You will be choosing two ANGEL Cards. The first Angel will assist you in realizing what is missing in the situation and how you became separate. The second Angel will support you in merging with the flow of the deeper process that is unfolding now.

Take a moment to welcome the presence of the Angels and bring your question to mind. When you feel ready, invite your first ANGEL Card to bring you insight into how the separateness happened. Then choose the second Angel to deepen your understanding of the unfolding process.

Now immediately go on a nature walk outside for a minimum of ten minutes. If you are in a city or urban area, the process is the same. The important part is that you go outside into the world. It is a silent expedition unless you meet someone who speaks to you first. Whatever captures your attention is part of your message in some way, even if it is a street sign or other object. The idea is that all that takes place is part of the answer and will reconnect you with the flow. Stay open and let the nature world speak to you.

As you walk, begin to connect with your first Angel and reflect on how the separateness occurred. What was the learning in the situation for you? Let the Angel show you the complete picture. For example, if you chose the Angel of Honesty, where did the truth get covered up? Or if you choose the Angel of Peace, what agitated you? Remember, each Angel holds the complete spectrum of the quality, including its opposite.

When you have completed the first part, invite your second Angel to be present. Allow your focus to soften; relax your mind and eyes. Take a few deeper breaths and open gently to the world around you. Walk for a few minutes, taking in nature. Feel the harmlessness of the birds and trees and the rhythm of life from their point of view. Then bring your Angel into your heart and merge with the quality; as you do, begin to look out your eyes through this quality. Note your thoughts and insights. Let your attention be drawn to a point of activity in front of you and recall your question. What does nature answer? What is the deeper rhythm that is seeking to emerge, and how can you best flow with it?

When you are finished, take time to journal your experience. As you write, stay open to additional insights and understandings. Give thanks to the Angels for their support, and release them with gratitude.

Use the Nature Walk Journal on page 62 to keep track of your experiences.

7

Using Journals With The ANGEL® Cards

Working in partnership with Angels is an exciting journey of self-discovery and love. We encourage you to keep a record of your experiences using the ANGEL Cards. Journaling provides a simple way of tracking and linking your intentions with your inner impressions and the outcomes that manifest.

You needn't write long explanations. A word or two can adequately acknowledge and encapsulate an experience. Simply notice and record whatever comes up for you without censoring, judging or analyzing.

Reviewing your journal entries will provide personal documentaion of the presence of spirit moving through your life, and valuable perspective on your unique cycles of change and development.

On the following pages are suggested journal formats for use with the ANGEL Cards meditations. Please feel free to copy these journal pages for your personal use.

ANGEL® Cards Journal

For use with Visualization (page 13),
Two-, Three-, Multi-card Spreads (pages 15-17),
and Weekly Meditation (page 49).

Date: _____

Intention: _____

_____

_____

Card(s) Selected: _____

_____

Message: _____

_____

_____

_____

_____

_____

Action: _____

_____

_____

_____

Relationship Angels Journal

For use with Relationship Meditation (page 50).

Date: _____

Relationship: _____

Intention: _____

_____

_____

Card Selected: _____

Insight: _____

_____

_____

_____

_____

Action: _____

_____

_____

_____

New Year Angels Journal

For use with New Year Meditation (page 51).

For the New Year: _____

Reflections of the Past Year: _____

_____

_____

_____

Intention #1: I intend to _____

_____

    Card Selected: _____

    Meaning: _____

    _____

Intention #2: I intend to _____

_____

    Card Selected: _____

    Meaning: _____

_____

Intention #3: I intend to _____

_____

    Card Selected: _____

    Meaning: _____

_____

Review Date: _____

Review intentions/resulting inspirations and insights: _____

_____

_____

Review Date: _____

Review intentions/resulting inspirations and insights: _____

_____

_____

Review Date: _____

Review intentions/resulting inspirations and insights: _____

_____

_____

Review Date: _____

Review intentions/resulting inspirations and insights: _____

_____

_____

Birthday Angels Journal

For use with Birthday Meditation (page 51).

For my _____ birthday

Reflections of the Past Year: _____

_____

_____

Intention #1: I intend to _____

_____

Card Selected: _____

Meaning: _____

_____

Intention #2: I intend to _____

_____

Card Selected: _____

Meaning: _____

_____

Intention #3: I intend to _____

_____

Card Selected: _____

Meaning: _____

_____

Review Date: _____

Review intentions/resulting inspirations and insights: _____

_____

_____

Review Date: _____

Review intentions/resulting inspirations and insights: _____

_____

_____

Review Date: _____

Review intentions/resulting inspirations and insights: _____

_____

_____

Review Date: _____

Review intentions/resulting inspirations and insights: _____

_____

_____

Nature Walk Journal

For use with Nature Walk Meditation (page 53).

Describe a situation in which you feel separateness: _____

_____

_____

_____

_____

_____

_____

Your question about the situation: _____

_____

_____

_____

_____

First Angel
(represents what is missing in the situation; how the separateness happened):

_____

Second Angel
(supports understanding and reconnection with the flow of the situation):

_____

What does nature answer?

_____

_____

_____

_____

_____

_____

_____

Insights and understandings:

_____

_____

_____

_____

_____

_____

_____

_____

_____

_____

Combination Blessing, Angel, and Insight Journal

For use with the exercise (page 18).

Date:

First focus area:

Blessing Cards:

What Blessing can I bring?

What Blessing will enhance my relationship?

ANGEL Card:

Insight Card:

Promptings:

Second focus area:

Blessing Cards:

What Blessing can I bring?

What Blessing will enhance my relationship?

ANGEL Card:

Insight Card: _____

_____

_____

Promptings: _____

_____

_____

Third focus area: _____

Blessing Cards: _____

    What Blessing can I bring? _____

    What Blessing will enhance my relationship? ____

ANGEL Card: _____

Insight Card: _____

_____

_____

Promptings: _____

_____

_____

8

Ongoing Work With The Angels

Continue to reflect on your Angel during your daily activity. Be alert to the ways your Angel shows up in these activities, either by expressing the quality yourself or by acknowledging another person who is expressing the quality.

Ask for a dream from your Angel to deepen your inner understanding of the quality. Write down whatever dream comes, even if it is not obvious at the time how it relates to your Angel.

Begin your day by reading the inspirational message for your chosen Angel from Chapter 5. Review the insight you received and take a few moments to reflect on your Angel again. Invite its presence and be open to it throughout your day. Reevaluate your action step and revise it if necessary.

Look up the keyword in the dictionary. This can give you a basic understanding of how the word has been used. The root and origin are sometimes very insightful.

Reflect on your interactions to gain insight into where and how the Angel has appeared in the past.

- Whom do you know who represents this Angel?
- What is it this person does, or how does he or she behave, that expresses this quality in a way that you would like to embody?
- Have you ever experienced this quality fully yourself?
- What was the underlying energy that allowed you to have that experience?

- How might you recreate that feeling in your life now?
- What actions can you take to bring this Angel into your relationships now?
- At the end of the day reflect on moments when this quality was present. How did the Angel show itself?

When you are finished working with your particular Angel, release it with your gratitude for its support and inspiration.

9

An Invitation To You

We would like to write a book based on inspirational experiences with the ANGEL® Cards. If you have an Angel story to tell or have experienced the support of the Angels as a result of using the ANGEL Cards and would like to share it, please write to us :

InnerLinks
P.O. Box 10502
Asheville, NC 28806 USA
Internet site: http://www.innerlinks.com
E-mail: angel@innerlinks.com

10

Resources

The Transformation Game®

The Transformation Game was created by Joy Drake and Kathy Tyler while living at the Findhorn Foundation. It captures the essence of the change process and puts it into a creative and insightful format that accelerates learning.

The game is a joyful and profound way of receiving insight at the deepest level, transforming the way you live your life. It is an excellent way to clarify important issues, resolve conflicts, and creatively enhance relationships. Through the game you can become more aware of personal strengths and learn important lessons that deepen your understanding of how you operate on the four levels of the game: Physical, Emotional, Mental, and Spiritual. The game can also be used as a powerful interactive tool, by both individuals and groups, for solving problems and achieving desired goals. By providing new perspectives on current life issues, the game helps you clarify old beliefs and attitudes, transforming your reaction patterns. The Transformation Game triggers creativity and the realization of your full power and potential.

The game offers a stimulating and informative context that encourages openness, cooperation, and sharing. It mirrors your life path and highlights your growing edge. It can provide clear feedback on the use of intuition and free will, helping to sharpen judgment, determine priorities, and build upon valuable resources within you. Through playing The Transformation Game, you may uncover and explore new dimensions and allow changes to occur in your life with greater understanding and ease.

The game is a multipurpose tool that can be experienced on many levels and has a variety of applications. It can be played just for fun or easily adapted by therapists, counselors, and professional facilitators to promote more in-depth experiences, for both individuals and groups.

The first version of the game was played in 1978 as part of the Art of Synthesis workshop. The game was held in the Cluny Hill College ballroom and played on a large path that filled the floor space with twenty participants and five facilitators. This version is still played and has evolved into the Planetary Game™. Other forms of the game also include The Game of Transformation and The Group Game™, described on pages 77 and 78.

Findhorn Foundation

The Findhorn Foundation is a spiritually-based educational community in northeast Scotland. It is recognized internationally for its cooperation with nature and promotion of the sacred in all that exists. There is no formal doctrine or creed; all the major world religions are honored and recognized as the many paths to God. An intentional community, Findhorn draws people from all walks of life who come to learn and practice their spiritual principles through their daily life in relationships, work, and concern for the Earth.

The community was founded in 1962 by Dorothy Maclean, Eileen Caddy, and Peter Caddy in a caravan park a mile from the seaside village of Findhorn. The founding principles included listening deeply to the God within and cooperating with nature as a creative force. What began as a garden quickly attracted the attention of individuals from all over the world who were interested in becoming divinely centered and of service to a vision for a positive future. Today the community is a developing eco-village with a thriving body of more than 350 people living and working together. The governing principles come from the body of people who live in the foundation. There is not a leader or teacher. All are encouraged to be accountable for their lifestyle.

The Findhorn Foundation is also an educational center that offers a wide variety of workshops and courses. Hundreds of guests come year 'round to participate in community life and engage with their personal and spiritual growth. Individuals can stay from a week to several months attending the various programs offered, such as community building, leadership, and the arts. The community is also actively engaged in environmental projects, including the construction of innovative ecological housing and the use of renewable energy systems. Recently the Findhorn Foundation has been granted Association with the Department of Public Information of the United Nations.

A number of organizations and businesses are either part of or associated with the Findhorn Foundation and the larger Findhorn Bay Community. An increasing number of people are gathering in the area to become part of this growing spiritual community and eco-village.

Meet the Creators of ANGEL® Cards

The creators of the ANGEL Cards, Joy Drake and Kathy Tyler, are the cofounders of InnerLinks Associates, a North Carolina-based international training and consulting company. They have extensive experience in the design, development, and delivery of products that catalyze creative changes: ANGEL Cards, Blessing Cards,™ The Transformation Game®, Intuitive Solutions®, and Frameworks for Change® Joy and Kathy teach facilitator trainings worldwide, and are Fellows of the Findhorn Foundation, Scotland.

Joy Drake

Joy Drake was on the faculty of the Findhorn Foundation from 1971 through 1985. During those years she held many positions and responsibilities, including Director of Internal Education, Director of Personnel, Admissions Officer, and Orientation Program Coordinator.

The Transformation Game began as a "hobby" in 1976, generated by Joy's desire to expand her inner life and share her knowledge of community building and service using spiritual principles. Using her own life as a crucible of experience, she was inspired to create a unique learning environment that enabled participants to accelerate changes in their lives through increased personal awareness and spiritual understanding.

Through Joy's willingness to work in cooperation with spirit and her dedication to personal and planetary transformation, The Transformation Game emerged as a remarkable catalyst for change.

Kathy Tyler

Kathy Tyler was on the faculty of the Findhorn Foundation from 1978 through 1985. As an educator and counselor she held positions in the Foundation as Chairperson of the Core Governing Group, Director of Personnel, and Staff Counselor to departments and project groups.

With a background in business management and as a meditation teacher, she came to the Foundation as the next step in her spiritual path. Kathy became involved with the creation of The Transformation Game in 1979. As a natural extension of her intuitive understanding of the evolutionary development of the human psyche, she contributed to the deeper understanding and inner workings of the process. Through her dedication and spiritual insight the game became a refined tool that demonstrates the power of personal accountability within the change process.

InnerLinks Associates

InnerLinks Associates is an international consulting and training company founded by Joy and Kathy in 1980 while they were living at the Findhorn Foundation. Since 1986 they have been living in the United States, where they research, develop, and market a range of innovative transformational tools. InnerLinks supports the outreach of various forms of The Transformation Game® and provides counseling, seminars, and training programs that encourage personal creativity, team learning, and organizational development. Joy and Kathy direct large, experiential group events for conferences and retreats. In 1992 they established a consulting practice using Frameworks for Change,® a business version of The Transformation Game. Both Kathy and Joy have served as adjunct faculty at Antioch University, Seattle, and the University of Washington.

InnerLinks continues to be affiliated with the Findhorn Foundation and maintains an office there. Mary Inglis, a member of the Foundation for over 25 years and a trustee for over 15 years, is a full partner and managing director of InnerLinks U.K. Mary leads courses and training programs in personal development and transformation, and she directs the outreach of InnerLinks throughout Europe, South Africa, and South America.

"InnerLinks specializes in helping individuals, teams, and organizations increase their understanding and experience of successful relationships and teamwork. Our approach uses sophisticated simulations that rapidly get to the root of real life challenges and facilitate intuitive solutions. The process pinpoints gaps where communication needs strengthening, reduces areas of weakness that undermine efforts and drain resources, and enhances valuable talents. Participants can access new ways of thinking and try out new behaviors. Each program stimulates the exchange of ideas and insights. Participants receive precise feedback, learn how to approach situations responsibly, and develop action steps they can take to improve their effectiveness and productivity. We offer a range of courses as well as certification and licensing programs."

Products

For deeper exploration into the Angels here are many of the products and services available to you.

ANGEL® Cards
The Original Angel Deck, Over 1 Million Decks Sold!

A set of 52 cards with playfully illustrated qualities inscribed, plus two blank cards for you to use creatively as you wish. An instruction sheet and convenient reusable carton are included. ANGEL Cards are available in several languages — English, Dutch, French, German, and Spanish.

ANGEL® Cards Inspirational Messages and Screensaver
Inspiring Software Programs

You can now choose ANGEL Cards from your personal computer. Pop-up windows for each card contain inspirational messages for insight and meditation. The software randomly deals a card or cards to your desktop. Your card or spread can stay on your desktop as a reminder throughout the day. A delightfully animated Screensaver program is also included in the package. Two 3.5″ discs for PCs running Windows 3.1 or Windows 95/98.

ANGEL® Stickers
Use Them Everywhere

A package of stickers contains two sets of 15 delightfully illustrated, self-adhesive paper ANGEL Stickers. You can use them to remember these special qualities in your life or to help you discover your own unique connection to the Angels. Put an ANGEL Sticker on your computer, the dashboard of your car, or the telephone, wherever you will see it frequently. Stick them on cards, presents, or packages and share them with friends and family.

ANGEL Companion™
Sterling Silver Pendant and Chain

A comforting presence for you or someone you care about, to remind you of the special help that is always available from the Angels. Choose an ANGEL Card as you wear your ANGEL Companion. Let it remind you of the current Angel quality that is supporting you. Actual height of the pendant is $\frac{3}{4}″$.

The Transformation Game®
For Two or More Players

A joyful and profound way to receive insight into our lives at the deepest level. The Transformation Game captures the essence of the change process and puts it into the delightful form of a board game that can be played with friends, family, or co-workers.

The game is an excellent way to clarify important issues, resolve conflicts, and creatively enhance relationships. Easy to play, the game requires no special training. It comes complete with playing instructions.

Solo And Earth Solo™
Supplement: for 1 player

Enjoy the benefits of The Transformation Game® in a solo setting. The Solo and Earth Solo supplement provides clarity on personal issues and gives you feedback on the impact of your actions, attitudes, and choices. Enhance your game experiences by using a meditative approach, playing at your own pace and recording your thoughts and feelings as your game progresses. The Transformation Game required; not included.

Intuitive Solutions®
A Tool for Inspired Action

A simple way to gain immediate clarity, understanding, motivation, inspiration, and direction. The Intuitive Solutions process is especially useful during a stressful period or transition, when you feel uncertain about your next step. Dive deeply into a concern, think through difficulties, and apply inner resources to make decisions in harmony with your values and integrity. You can use Intuitive Solutions to assist you to break through blocks to creativity, change an unproductive behavior, heal a relationship, or fulfill your deepest desire. It is a wonderful tool for navigating life's ups and downs and strengthens your ability to turn insights into effective actions. A boxed set of Insight and Setback Cards adapted from The Transformation Game and a deck of ANGEL® Cards plus instruction book. For 1 or more players.

Blessing Cards™
Blessings for You and the Earth

A product of The Transformation Game, the Blessings pack comes with over 200 colorful cards describing qualities such as Reassurance, Vitality, Fulfillment, Dependability, and Absurdity. Blessings make wonderful, spontaneous gifts, can add brightness and sparkle to your day, and give you insights into challenging situations. Place them in a bowl on your desk or table and offer a blessing to all you meet. Use your imagination to come up with new ways to play.

Services

Transformation Game® Facilitators Training

Whether you would like to offer Transformation Game workshops professionally or take the game to a deeper level with friends, this intensive program gives you a thorough training in the use of the game with an advanced manual. Accreditation as a facilitator for the game allows you to promote workshops using The Transformation Game, with InnerLinks' formal permission given only to those who successfully complete the training.

Frameworks for Change®

A specialized version of The Transformation Game for use in business settings, Frameworks for Change is a sophisticated simulation that can stimulate the honest exchange of ideas and insights, develop intuitive decision-making skills, and rapidly get to the root of challenges. The process focuses on the intrinsic personal value of work, bringing meaning to what we do with a sense of accomplishment and worth. For those who want to expand their facilitation skills and work with the Frameworks for Change model in organizations, InnerLinks offers a certification program suitable for consultants, organizational development specialists, coaches, and trainers who have a diverse, active client base.

Transformational Conference Events

We customize Frameworks for Change or The Transformation Game for large conferences to encourage participant interaction. These events can offer the opportunity to focus specifically on conference-related themes and collectively reshape individual and global concerns.

The Planetary Game™

The Planetary Game is a life-sized version of The Transformation Game that weaves together the creative elements of ritual and innovative group work in a sacred theater setting. It provides an exciting, multidimensional environment in which clarity, insight, and healing are brought to areas of personal and planetary concern, serving as an anchor for new hope and vision. The Planetary Game is for those who are longing to reconnect deeply and intimately with their own being and to recognize how they impact, and are influenced by, the transformative dynamics arising in the individual and collective psyche.

The Game of Transformation™

Just as life is filled with a rich variety of experiences, so is The Game of Transformation. Facilitated by two professionally trained guides, the game involves five players and centers on a board symbolizing each player's world. As you move along your path, you gain a wider perspective on your own particular patterns of behaviors and attitudes. The game offers you the opportunity to recognize your strengths, review and resolve challenges, and explore new ways of interacting. The Game of Transformation™ is a playful yet substantial way of understanding and transforming key life issues.

Group Game™

The Group Game provides a context in which personal awareness, group work, and spiritual growth are magnified and quickened. Individual insight and learning are inevitable through this version of The Transformation Game®. As it is played on more than the personal level, an experience of group consciousness emerges as the game unfolds. The direct impact of our decisions on the environment around us is revealed. By engaging in mindful play together, we can explore our interconnectedness in tangible and practical ways, resulting in the realization of our potential to effect change in ourselves, our groups, and our world.

Intuitive Coaching™

Kathy Tyler offers Intuitive Coaching using meditative inquiry. This process opens a window into the unconscious, revealing the invisible energetic patterns operating at deep levels within the psyche. During the session we explore together the contributing factors and influences that shape your outer experience. You emerge from the session with a clear sense of specific dynamics and simple, key steps to make positive changes and to evoke healing. Telephone consultation is available.

11

Contact Information

InnerLinks

If you are interested in the products and services InnerLinks offers, please contact:

InnerLinks USA
P.O. Box 10502
Asheville, NC 28806 USA
Phone: 828-665-9937
Fax: 828-665-9957
Internet site: http://www.innerlinks.com
E-mail: angel@innerlinks.com

InnerLinks UK
Findhorn Foundation
Forres IV36 3TZ Scotland
Phone/Fax: +44 (0)1309 690 992
E-mail: minglis@findhorn.org

Findhorn Foundation

If you are interested in more information or would like to receive a brochure, please contact:

Findhorn Foundation
Administration
The Park, Findhorn
Forres IV36 3TZ Scotland
Phone: +44 (0)1309 691 620
Fax: +44 (0)1309 691 663
Internet site: http://www.findhorn.org
E-mail: reception@findhorn.org

Music Design

ANGEL® products are available at fine book and gift stores everywhere. Ask your retailer to order them for you. If you have trouble locating them, contact Music Design, the exclusive distributor of ANGEL products.

ANGEL Products Department
Music Design, Inc.
4650 N. Port Washington Road
Milwaukee, WI 53212 USA
Phone: 800-862-7232 Monday through Friday, 8:30 a.m. to 5:30 p.m. CST, United States and Canada.
For calls outside the US and Canada, please dial: 414-961-8380
FAX (24 hours, 7 days): 414-961-8381
E-mail: order@musicdesign.com
Internet site: http://www.musicdesign.com/AngelCard.html

12

Acknowledgements

We appreciate the Angels who have been our
brilliant, firm, and steady companions.

We would like to thank all those people who have encouraged us to go forward with our vision of positive transformation. It has been a life-changing journey that has challenged and enriched us.

We are grateful to those of you who use the ANGEL® Cards and share them with friends and family. Thank you for your inspiration and support.

And, of course, huge thanks to the Narada Productions staff, especially Anne Aufderheide and Wesley Van Linda, for continually holding the ANGEL Cards with integrity and with conscious appreciation for the role and value of spirit in business.